FIND THE WAY!

FIND THE WAY!

*More Stories of Yates,
the Guide Dog
with a Dog Collar*

Mike Endicott

Terra Nova Publications

© Mike Endicott 2002

First published by Terra Nova Publications Ltd, 2002

All rights reserved.

Mike Endicott asserts the moral right
to be identified as the author of this work.

No part of this publication may be reproduced or
transmitted in any form or by any means, electronic
or mechanical, including photocopy, recording or any
information storage and retrieval system, without
permission in writing from the publisher.

Published in Great Britain by
Terra Nova Publications Ltd
PO Box 2400, Bradford on Avon, Wiltshire BA15 2YN

Scripture quotations taken from the
Holy Bible, New International Version. Copyright
© 1973, 1978, 1984 by International Bible Society.
Used by permission of Hodder and Stoughton Ltd.
All rights reserved.

ISBN 1901949168

Line drawing by Amanda Endicott

Printed in Great Britain by Cox & Wyman, Reading

Contents

	Foreword	7
	Introduction	9
1.	Golden Apples, Greasy Beefburgers	11
2.	The Dog and the Frog	17
3.	The Blocked Path	21
4.	The Gardener	27
5.	The Television Studio	33
6.	Heads in the Sand	39
7.	Loneliness	43
8.	Slippery Character	51
9.	The Harvester	55
10.	Pastimes	61
11.	Control	69
12.	Devious Devices	75
13.	Steal Away	81
14.	Getting a Lift	85
15.	Adoption	89

Foreword

Over the last few years, I have heard Mike telling lots of stories about the adventures he and Yates have had together. They are often very funny, and always fascinating, but they are also something more. As Mike explains the unique relationship of trust that exists between himself and Yates, he uses it to show us how God longs for a similar kind of relationship with us. It astounds me to discover just how many things Mike is able to do, and how many places he is able to visit, simply because of Yates, but all this is only possible because of the way they trust and rely on one another. And, of course, the trust and reliance only comes because they also respect and love one another deeply. Watching the way that Yates and Mike become one, as they stride off together through crowded streets, always gives me a kick.

Mike has told me of the closeness that exists between him and Yates: "When he's got his harness on, he thinks I'm actually part of his own body!" —and he speaks of the way he himself has to keep very close to the Lord, in order to minister effectively to the people he meets each day.

Yes, this is a profound book, but it is also great fun, easy to read, and a fascinating account of the complex, demanding and extremely responsible job of being a guide dog. I know you are going to enjoy it on many different levels, but to get the very best out of it, do let it speak to you on the deepest level of all.

Jennifer Rees Larcombe

Introduction

This book is a collection of short stories about my daily life with a guide dog. The stories vary from the thoughtful to the hilarious, but each has a message embedded within it about the deeper things of life.

Whether the reader loves dogs or God (or both, as I do) it is hoped that, within these pages, the dog-lover may learn something of God, and the God worshipper may increase in his knowledge and understanding of dogs!

My guide dog, Yates, is my premier mobility aid, but he is also one of my closest friends. The partnership between us is very precious—it brings a sort of new joy and freedom into my world as a visually impaired person. The bond between a guide dog owner and dog is terribly special and close. It seems to involve a deep kind of communication, perhaps, in part, because of whatever these dogs have inherited through their hunting wolf-pack generational history.

I have always loved dogs and I come from a family

background which was full of pets; but my relationship with Yates is stronger than it has been with any other dog I have ever known.

In my book *Trust Yates!*, Yates and I had been a partnership for two and a half years. We had grown to be inseparable. Now, two years on, there have continued to be many hilarious occasions in our everyday lives together, as well as some more thought-provoking ones, each a little story in itself.

Of course, Yates does not actually converse in English with me—the words I credit him with in this book, as in *Trust Yates!*, are spoken only in my imagination. Being without sight means that I miss most of his body language, too. I have had to rely on the comments of family and friends to fill in the picture. Nevertheless, he has continued to teach me a great deal.

1
Golden Apples, Greasy Beefburgers

A word aptly spoken is like apples of gold in settings of silver.
Proverbs 25:11

The spatial awareness or 'measuring' ability of guide dogs is so amazing that you might imagine they had studied mathematics!

Yates did not just arrive at home, waiting to leap into harness and be the impressive animal that he is—he had been trained, and that training process has equipped him well for the things he has to do. It is not only the dog that needs teaching — the would-be handler has to undergo some three or four weeks of residential training to handle such a finely tuned beast. I cannot say that I enjoyed that experience!

Trusting a dog to keep one safe can only be learned by encouragement and practice. The encouragement is very interesting, but the practice is frightening. Being out and

FIND THE WAY!

alone with a dog in harness for the first time, not being able to see a hand in front of one's face in a busy shopping street, is not exactly fun. The rewards are enormous, though: freedom, independence and unconditional love; but getting there is not so easy! The new guide dog owner has to learn to trust and encourage the dog, who needs to do exactly the same to this new master.

Where does mathematics come in? For weeks I wondered and pondered on the question, "How does he know about gaps?" When he and I are out on the open road, we find many obstacles that have to be measured before any attempt to negotiate them is made. There are lamp posts, ice cream signs, parked cars, railings, narrow doorways and a thousand others. Gaps of all widths have to be measured in advance for Yates to decide whether we are going through, or whether he should take some sort of evasive action and go around. How does he do that? How does he work out the danger? Each of these decisions is taken some six or seven yards away, so that Yates does not jerk me about through last minute decision-making. He looks; he measures; he decides.

I spent the first four weeks of our relationship wondering whether he says to himself, "Now, up ahead is a wall on my left and a lamp post on my right. I'm about nine inches across the shoulders, Dad is a little more than that. There are about four or five inches between us and, if I add all those measurements together, do I get a figure which is greater than that gap up ahead? Hang on, there's a lady walking towards us! If she gets into the gap before we do, my measurements will all be up the creek! Well, I suppose we might make it, as long as that car door doesn't open...."

GOLDEN APPLES, GREASY BEEFBURGERS

Although Yates might well qualify for the finals of any Worldwide Wonderful Wagger Competition, he is not that clever —he has no idea about mathematics! Well, he is not stupid, either. Making decisions at some distance from the object in question, so as not to jerk Dad too much, enables him to line up on some child's discarded beefburger at twenty paces and stride purposefully and smoothly straight over the top of it. As his front feet become level with this object of deep desire, his head drops, grabs and lifts again with a viper strike that defies any attempt on my part to correct him. It is all over in a flash!

After a month of intrigued debate going on in my mind, I decided to approach one of the trainers and ask the question, "How does he measure gaps?"

The trainer's answer plunged into my brain and locked itself into my memory —never, I hope, to be dislodged. It was such a godly answer! It went a long way to sum up for me in that moment, and in one sentence, the whole doctrine of atonement. "You see," said the trainer, "when you are both together, he thinks that you and he are one."

At that point in our history of working together, I began to feel a bond beginning to form which has deepened considerably over the intervening years. What links us together is not so much a harness, or some sort of co-dependency, but mutual encouragement. Since that early moment of realisation, when the light dawned for me on Yates' workings, encouragement has been the key to our relationship. I build him up with excited words, titbits and ear rubs, while he encourages me with nose pushing. From time to time, when he is not working in harness or lazing around in the garden, Yates will walk over to me, sometimes when I am working in the office, push his nose up into the palm of one hand and watch me as if to ask, "Everything OK, Dad?" This is encouragement through caring.

In the Old Testament is the story of Naaman, who was the commander of the Syrian army. He was a great man in the opinion of the king and highly regarded in the country. He was a brave and valiant soldier, but, unhappily, he had leprosy.

A servant girl in his house said to her mistress, "If only my master would see the prophet who is in Samaria! He would cure him of his leprosy."

So, after many twists and turns in the story, Naaman travelled down to Samaria with his horses and chariots and stopped at the door of Elisha the prophet.

Elisha sent a messenger to say to him, "Go, wash yourself seven times in the Jordan, and your flesh will be restored and you will be cleansed." Eventually Naaman did just that and was healed. Like so many Bible stories, this one is full of lessons, but think about what an encouragement this was for the messenger. Ministry to others in the Christian Church is like the role of a messenger or postman. God produces all the 'parcels', but uses men and women to deliver them to the would-be recipients; and so many of us would love to be used more and more in this way.

How encouraging and thrilling it must have been for Elisha's messenger to know that not only did the 'boss' trust him with an errand, but it worked! The word of God, the message delivered, had a positive result. Surely he must have been so uplifted in his soul.

Life is filled with plenty of negative thoughts, events and set-backs. We all need a word of encouragement.

Perhaps we should set out to give such an encouraging word to at least one person every day, to people of all ages. It may very well be the best gift we can give to anyone!

> The LORD your God is with you,
> he is mighty to save.
> He will take great delight in you,
> he will quiet you with his love,
> he will rejoice over you with singing.
>
> *Zephaniah 3:17*

What a wonderful concept to try to grasp! God is rejoicing over each one of us with gladness and with singing. What an amazing thing that is! He loves us that much. He sees our failures, all our faults, and he loves us still. To him, each of us is a precious person, worth singing and rejoicing over.

Often, our human tendency is to remember our mistakes, and to wonder how God could love us when we seem to fall so short of any reasonable target, most of the time.

As God looks upon us, he sees his creation, and each of us is special to him. It is not that his love is divided equally among all of us, but that his entire love is directed at each individual.

He is not waiting for our weakest moment, when we are beaten into the ground, to drag out a long list of our mistakes and lecture us about them, one by one. Once they have been forgiven, they are forgotten, and our God will quiet us with his love. We do well to remember that as we fall short yet again, then repent, and are cleansed by the blood of Jesus, our heavenly Father rejoices over us 'with

FIND THE WAY!

singing'. How special we are to him, and how endless is his love!

2

The Dog and the Frog

As you go, preach this message: 'The kingdom of heaven is near.' Heal the sick, raise the dead, cleanse those who have leprosy, drive out demons. Freely you have received, freely give.
Matthew 10:7–8

We stood watching Yates for about twenty minutes. He was completely oblivious to our presence—sitting quietly in the Easter sunshine at the edge of the fishpond and staring down into its depths. He was transfixed.

Every thirty seconds or so, he threw out a front paw and scooped up the surface of the water. Then he sat for a while longer, silently staring down into a sea of apparent fascination as the flickering sunlight died away on the fading ripples.

I whispered his name. Up came the great black head to glance fleetingly in our direction, but his concentration was unbroken. He ignored me and returned to watch the water.

FIND THE WAY!

Ginnie, my wife, quietly strolled over and stood closer, in the hope of sharing in whatever this adventure was. Stepping gently back from the edge, so as not to break his stare of concentration, she said, "It's a big frog! He wants the frog to come out to play, but she won't come. It's because it's a sunny day, I suppose. Frogs like to be in the water when it's dry on the bank."

We walked back up the garden in the evening sunshine, leaving Yates to go on encouraging the reluctant frog to leave its watery home and play with him. Poor old Yates would be so disappointed if she did not. Five minutes later, he wandered heavily back along the path to the back door, disheartened, head down and dispirited. How he had longed for the frog to come out and play!

I knew how Yates felt, standing still at the side of the pond in the fading evening light. This is an apt picture of what it feels like to preach at a healing service, get to the end of the talk, and then call people to approach the front, to receive ministry. For many years, there seemed to be a never-ending gap at the conclusion of each sermon or seminar talk that I gave; then the optimistic few would struggle up towards me, heads bowed, in reverent quiet. How I longed for them to push and crowd joyfully towards the front, yearning to bathe in the sunshine of God's gracious healing favour.

There is a pool in Jerusalem called Bethesda, which is surrounded by five covered colonnades. A considerable number of disabled people used to lie around the pool, waiting for what they understood to be the right moment. There Jesus found a man who had been an invalid for thirty-eight years.

> When Jesus saw him lying there and learned that he had been in this condition for a long time, he asked him, "Do you want to get well?"
>
> "Sir," the invalid replied, "I have no-one to help me into the pool when the water is stirred. While I am trying to get in, someone else goes down ahead of me."
>
> *John 5:6–7*

Jesus' response was apparently a simple one: "Get up! Pick up your mat and walk."

Notice that the invalid was trying to set the agenda. He had in mind a set method which was the accepted way of doing things, as far as he was concerned. He was also having a grumble!

Jesus did not want to get involved in all the techniques; he seemed uninterested in the 'ceremonial' traditions. His answer was short and sweet, cutting through the grumbly, ritualistic rigmarole: "Get up! Pick up your mat and walk." Those who minister in Jesus' name today long for people to give up the 'Ah, buts', jump out of the murky waters of ritualistic tradition once in a while, and just enjoy the grace of God together!

Three nights after Yates' fruitless wait for the frog to join in with him, it rained. It poured and bucketed down, and Yates lay curled up in his bed, refusing to be remotely interested in anything. His bed is in the utility room, in such a position that, without moving, he can watch two ways. More importantly, he can see what goes on in the kitchen through the glass separating door, and he can also keep a watchful eye down the garden, through the back door. The more the rain came down, the tighter he curled up in bed. Ginnie went past him and opened the door, only to squeal with delight: "It's the frog from the pond! She's come to fetch Yates out to play!"

Sure enough, there was the frog, sitting on the back doorstep, staring in through the open door at the uninterested black lump in the dog bed. Yates turned slowly and his head rested on the edge of the bed, one eye on the frog, one on the raindrops, and one eyebrow raised in disbelief. 'How could anybody in their right mind think it would be fun to go out and play on a night like this?'

I tried to encourage Yates: "If at first you don't succeed, it's always worth persevering with others—you never know when they will change their minds, and come and join in!"

God has taught me, both in experience and his word, that perseverance is vital for all Christians who want to be effective in the kingdom. Never be discouraged by the 'frog-like' tendencies of so many folk, who seem to reject you or your love for the Lord. Be patient; and, unlike Yates, be ready for the response when it does come!

3

The Blocked Path

You have declared this day that the LORD is your God and that you will walk in his ways, that you will keep his decrees, commands and laws, and that you will obey him. And the LORD has declared this day that you are his people, his treasured possession as he promised, and that you are to keep all his commands.

Deuteronomy 26:17–18

It was late one evening. Yates and I were walking along the same route we always take, through the local town. I began to notice that unwelcome little autumn chill that creeps into the evening air, heralding the end of summer. But Yates' tail was swinging with an easy rhythm and we were picking up speed, happy after a rewarding day. Our blood circulations were working well, and we swung along with the usual high expectancy as we headed for home.

I had been caught up with some wonderful times of prayer, worship and teaching during the day, and Yates had begged one or two biscuits and slept a great deal —so, in different ways, we both felt fulfilled as we increased the pace in order to keep warm.

Past the shops and over the road bridge we strode, down the ramp and around the corner to the bottom of the hill. From there, our route turns ninety degrees to the right, onto a tarmac path with high brick walls on either side. Another quarter of a mile and we would be at the traffic lights. From there we only had to climb the hill on the other side of the valley, and we would be home— within reach of the kettle, central heating radiators and a tempting dog bed for Yates!

Five paces around the corner, Yates threw out all four anchors, stopping in his tracks and jerking me to a shaking halt. What was he keeping me from? Tentatively, I slid one foot forward, to see if the ground had collapsed in front of us, but there was smooth tarmac ahead for at least one pace. Stepping to the left and the right, I stretched out a hand and found the brick walls on either side of the path. So what was stopping him? "Come on, old man," I suggested somewhat forcefully. "It's getting cold, and I want to go home!" He refused to budge an inch. Gingerly stepping forward two more paces, I reached out in front of me as far as I could, and there it was —a wall-to-wall chain link fence as tall as me, blocking the path. What a total surprise; we had never expected this!

As we stood there in the icy draught which funnelled its way between the high, brick walls, Yates waited patiently for the next instruction, while I had an unexpected flashback. I remembered far off days when our boys were small and one of our greatest challenges was getting them off to sleep at night. If we ourselves reach

THE BLOCKED PATH

out for long-dimmed memories, and recall what it was like to be little children, we can understand why getting to sleep is so hard sometimes! Firstly, I remember one particular prayer learned in Sunday School, which never works: "Now I lay me down to sleep; I pray the Lord my soul to keep." So far, so good, but then: "If I should die before I wake...." That last line is enough. No half intelligent child with even a scrap of imagination is going to go to sleep after that! They might never wake up again!

There is another reason why little boys find it hard to get to sleep sometimes: the 'monster in the wardrobe'. Parents never really seem to understand that, once the light goes out, a really scary and blood-thirsty monster wakes up inside the wardrobe, just a few feet from the end of the bed. So, they lie there with their eyes wide open, afraid of what that monster might do to them as soon as they fall asleep. Then there is the frightening possibility of the arrival of more imagined creatures: half-human, half blood-sucking vampires, flying in through the open window yet invisible in mirrors! They creep silently up behind you and bite you on the neck. Why do parents always insist on leaving the bedroom window on the latch? There is nothing else for it but to sit bolt upright and stare at the window, not even blinking in case the vital moment of the vampire's arrival is missed!

We may all be grown up now, but this chain link fence reminded me of something—there is still a 'monster in our wardrobe' that makes it very hard to live in peace. This threatening creature is not an imaginary one. Like the chain link fence, it is all too real—one of life's ultimate, inevitable realities: "If I should die before I wake...." The monster of death comes out of the wardrobe every time we have to attend a funeral, and it creeps up really close to us if the person who has died was somewhere around our own age. One day, surely, it will be me in that coffin. What is more, the longer we live, the quicker the years seem to slip past us. One of these fine days, the 'monster' of death will catch all of us. Out there, beyond our last heartbeat, is a lot of unknown terrain; we have no natural knowledge of what it feels or looks like, but there is one thing we do know about it: we leave this life for ever.

Only God can speak with absolute authority about death. Only he knows what lies in wait for us beyond the moment of our death, and he has given us very good news about the 'monster' that lurks in our imagination. Hebrews 2:14–15 says:

> Since the children have flesh and blood, he [Jesus] too shared in their humanity so that by his death he might destroy him who holds the power of death—that is, the devil—and free those who all their lives were held in slavery by their fear of death.

'Their fear of death'? This shutting-off of this life at the end is inevitable, and it is natural to feel that we do not know where it will take us. However, it is possible to 'find the way'. I think of how putting my life in the hands of a trained and caring dog removes my fear of being lost. On a very much deeper level, putting our life into the hands of Jesus Christ liberates us from the fear of death. Why? Because we then know, for sure, that death for us will mean heaven forever. The 'monster in the wardrobe' was put to death when Jesus died on the cross. How can I guarantee that? The only way is to have the 'chain link fence' that could keep me out of God's heaven—my sins—removed forever by Jesus Christ.

There was no way through the fence in front of us, that had stopped Yates in his tracks, and there is no way for us to enter heaven with our sins. They form a barrier to our enjoying a close walk with God as our heavenly Father—a wonderful relationship which is his best will and purpose for us. There is only one person who can forgive sins—Jesus, who died to pay for them, to wash us clean and free us from them. He tasted death for everyone. He made atonement for our sins; they have been paid for—and we never have to pay again, if we give ourselves to him. Beyond death will be eternal life in heaven. But if we have never totally trusted Jesus as our Saviour from our sin, we are depending upon our own righteousness instead, and that will never be enough; depending on our own merits, we would always fall short of holiness. Until we meet, accept and receive Jesus as Saviour and Lord, we can never completely be free from the fear that haunts so many people throughout their lives. Then, and only then, can we know for certain that if we 'die before we wake', we will be in heaven forever with him.

So what would Yates and I do about a very practical problem? This was our route home. We had never previously taken any other way back to the house. I had a vague idea of the direction, but that was all. Jesus had rescued me from a dead-end road, so many years earlier. Now I wondered if a guide dog could get me home that evening. "Find the way, Yates!" I commanded, with authority in my voice, but some uncertainty in my thoughts. That particular command is the one of last resort. When all seems lost and the way ahead is too uncertain and risky, the only thing a guide dog owner can do is throw his own sovereignty to the wind and let the real boss take the reins. This was what he had been waiting for, so patiently. Yates spun me around, with the self-assured, military precision of someone who knows exactly what he is doing and has done many times before. Back around the sharp corner we had just negotiated, up the slope—and then, to my surprise, straight on. To have turned right would have been a natural route for him to have taken—that is the way we go to work. He had never gone straight on before; this was completely new territory for him. Without a second's pause for thought, Yates struck out diagonally across the square to the long steps over in the far corner. How did he know they were there? He had never been to this square before!

Down the concrete stairway at the back of the Magistrates' Court we went, round the side of the building, across a car park —and then we stopped again. Was he lost? Had he stopped out of confusion, being somewhere far from home that he did not recognise?

It was then that I heard a friendly, helpful voice: "Can I help you, sir?" I had been worrying much more than Yates —he had brought me to the bottom step of the entrance to the police station! After that, all was plain sailing; we were safe. I had asked Yates to do what he knows how to do best—and he brought us safely home.

Yates knew whom he could rely upon. *We* each need to come to know Jesus for ourselves; he is the one to whom we can call for help, and depend on totally:

> Salvation is found in no-one else, for there is no other name under heaven given to men by which we must be saved.
>
> *Acts 4:12*

4

The Gardener

For when we were controlled by the sinful nature, the sinful passions aroused by the law were at work in our bodies, so that we bore fruit for death. But now, by dying to what once bound us, we have been released from the law so that we serve in the new way of the Spirit, and not in the old way of the written code.

Romans 7:5–6

Sunny sabbaths in February are not two a penny, and such enjoyable opportunities have to be grasped with open arms. The last one of these that came our way shone through the back door into Yates' bed and warmed him temptingly into considering a not-so-early morning stroll in the garden.

This, of course, would have to be a post-breakfast expedition — Yates cannot be motivated into anything at all before eating. He seems to find that a full stomach stimulates all sorts of interests, but an empty one only makes for big eyes and raised eyebrows!

Second only to eating, being offered the 'play' collar is

enough to push him over the brink into wide-awake consciousness. Bells jangling, he shot down the garden path as if in pursuit of a fleeing postman, leaving me to struggle along in his wake, hoping to discover what the day would have in store for us both.

At the bottom end of the sweeping lawn, beyond the old brick bird-bath and the overhanging willow, stand a number of silver birch trees, and I finished up among them, feeling with outstretched hands the pleasure of creation along their branches and the bumpy bark.

To my dismay, four of the smaller ones were covered with ivy. "Yates," I informed him of my decision, "this lot will have to come off!"

He dutifully followed me back and forth in a zigzag search pattern behind the apple trees, until we found the wheelbarrow and then, armed with a pair of secateurs, we set out to bring freedom to the trees. Well, that was what I thought we were doing.

Ripping, tearing and cutting the ivy from the branches, I piled it, by the armful, into the barrow and pushed it flat, wondering all the time why I had not yet filled it and had to make the inevitable trip to the rubbish dump in the far bottom corner of the garden. What a wonderful wheelbarrow: it never overflowed!

Then I heard it. Having turned to grapple yet again with a resisting ivy stem that had wound itself so tightly around a branch that it now seemed to be a component part of the tree, I heard the distinct sound of a guide dog climbing out of a plastic wheel barrow. As I turned to protest, the bells on the play collar gave the game away as Yates sprang down, pulling masses of the horrible stuff out onto the lawn. It would seem that I had struck a problem. Yates and I were in basic disagreement about all this. In my gardening ignorance, I had supposed that ivy should be pulled off its intended victim and removed to some place of safe-keeping, preferably where it would remain for ever, eventually to rot down. Yates, on the other hand, had apparently decided that these long bits of green rope with leaves on, together with the lovely whippy bits that flapped around his ears when shaken from side to side with gusto and delight, must have been designed for his pleasure alone, and needed rescuing from a master who did not quite seem to understand this.

We may have grudges like that pile of ivy: sometimes, as hard as we might try to get rid of them, they do not go away. From somewhere, buried in the memories of an earlier time, there leapt up in front of me a wonderful newspaper cartoon, one of those that lurk in the back of the mind for a whole life span because they struck some now long forgotten chord at the time. The drawing depicted a man struggling to chop down a vine which was threatening to take over the outside of his house. It had thoroughly entwined and entangled itself around his ankles, trapping him against the wall. From somewhere around the back of the house snaked yet another wriggling and serpent-like vine tentacle. Watching from the front door, his wife shouted, "Look out, Henry! Here it comes again!"

I stepped towards Yates and fell straight into an ivy pile as deep as my knees. So many of us cannot openly admit, even to ourselves, that we have a grudge or two that keep doing this to us. Again and again, they come shooting at us out of nowhere, getting tangled around our spiritual ankles until we trip and tumble down, furious and frustrated that we have fallen for that one again. Then there are some times when these returning grudges do not feel ivy-like at all, but much more like a stocky, heavy, over-enthusiastic black Labrador that keeps wanting to leap into one's arms!

We keep trying to hand these grudges over to God, asking, "Excuse me, God, please will you look after this and somehow dissolve it away? I'm just a miserable sinner and I can't seem to deal with this one." Often, it seems that the grudge then flies away for a while. Our prayers have been answered; our confession has worked. Then it comes back when we are not looking!

We Christians are supposed to forgive as much as we want to be forgiven. On many occasions we know that we have forgiven worse offences against us than whatever it is at the epicentre of a particular grudge. For whatever might turn out to be the true reason, we sometimes find it very hard to release lasting forgiveness. This can be really annoying, especially when bigger problems have been dealt with successfully; it is the smaller, whippy ones that keep coming back! We may never have been able to find a way of properly resolving some old anger about whatever it was that happened, try as we may. We frequently manage to forget about it for long periods of time; but then, suddenly, there it is again, as though it has spent time just lurking out of sight around the corner of the house, ready to pounce. We might feel like stamping like an irate child on that old unsolved problem, as if it were a sheet of bubble wrap, or a frozen puddle on the pavement. Whatever the root, our anger is still ours to manage; it is there; still 'our' problem, and the truth is that only God can help us deal with it.

Peter seems to have had such a struggle:

THE GARDENER

> Then Peter came to Jesus and asked, "Lord, how many times shall I forgive my brother when he sins against me? Up to seven times?"
>
> Jesus answered, "I tell you, not seven times, but seventy-seven times."
>
> *Matthew 18:21–22*

The expression 'seventy-seven times', and, elsewhere, 'seven times seventy', signifies acts of unconditional forgiveness as often as needed. Each time we speak out into the heavenlies our intention to forgive, a little piece of us becomes a little more healed. The fact is that we have to persevere in forgiving. Even if we don't *feel* like forgiving, we are to do so as an act of the will, a decision. God honours such a step of obedience. The next time we think of that person it will be with a slightly less earth-trembling shudder. When we speak again about them, it will be without poison in what we say. When we hear again of them, we may be able to hear something 'nice' for a change. When we next see them in the street, we will be just that little bit slower to cross over and avoid them. Every act of forgiveness yields healing. The terrible truth is that unwillingness to forgive is self-destructive, in all kinds of ways. By remaining in a position of unforgiveness, we really do harm ourselves. This is abundantly clear to anyone involved in the Christian healing ministry.

Unable to convince Yates of the correct procedure for ivy removal, I switched my attention to a winter-fallen branch that had earlier cost me a twisted ankle, and was destined to be burned on the bonfire. Picking up the thick end under one arm, I dragged it to the edge of the drive, but then it became jammed —between the weeping willow and the old brick bird-bath underneath it, I supposed.

Placing the heavy end on the grass, I worked my way back up its full length, hand over hand, until my palm fell onto a wet black nose surmounting a dazzling white smile. Would I ever win?

5

The Television Studio

And we, who with unveiled faces all reflect the Lord's glory, are being transformed into his likeness with ever-increasing glory, which comes from the Lord, who is the Spirit.

2 Corinthians 3:18

A television quiz show? A panel game? Yates and I looked at each other while I offered the letter of invitation from the producer in his direction.

Yates appeared thoughtful, or so it seemed. A guide dog, after all, has his 'street cred' to take care of. If a dog has to be involved in the religious life, we could, at the very least, have been invited to take part in some deeply theological or spiritual discussion. One of those popular cookery programmes would have even greater possibilities! I could almost hear Yates selecting the latter as the best choice —a dog could really savour that idea!

"They're offering to pay us a fee!" I told him. So, on the appointed day, we duly arrived at the studio. Yates, as

FIND THE WAY!

I thought, would have been far happier with a cookery show. He displayed his contempt for the proceedings so overtly that I found it quite embarrassing.

The studio staff had built up three or four layers of staging boxes alongside my chair, and had thrown a red cloth over the top. Their intention was that a full frontal camera shot of our team would show not only the three human contestants but a guide dog in line on the end. Our team captain would then introduce us as a four-man team that week! But Yates did not think this was very funny. There is, after all, quite a difference between having stardom thrust upon one and letting it grow under proper guide dog control. So, just as the rehearsal began, he stood up, turned around and lay down again, presenting a great black backside to the cameras. This, it would seem, is the most obvious way of showing guide dog contempt—both for the proceedings and at having his dignity so reduced.

"Cut!" shouted some earnest voice beyond the bright studio lights. Tightening Yates' lead, I fought manfully for a few seconds to turn him round. The struggle was much like trying to turn over a sack of wet potatoes at arm's length, and all to no avail. He had just drifted off to sleep and was not about to perform for his anxious owner. Happily, a solution to the problem was on the way in the shape and form of the studio director. Very quietly he said to Yates, "Yates, old boy, I wonder if you would mind sitting up and turning round, so that I can get the camera...." The mention of the word 'camera' was enough. Yates shot to his feet, swivelled around, and sat down again, head erect and pointing first to one side and then the other. Which would be his best angle?

Now that we were all lined up correctly, the shooting of

the rehearsal began. Our team lost this rehearsal game by thousands of points and all four of us beat a glum retreat to the hospitality suite.

I had really wanted to use this opportunity to reflect the light of Christ through people's television sets into their homes somehow, but losing heavily did not really fit in with my plans!

As we waited to appear before the television audience in the studio, I began to think about what this 'reflecting his light' really means. Perhaps it was Yates' 'vanity' that reminded me of how self-centred it is possible to become, even when what we *really* want to do is to shine for Jesus. As St. Paul asked, 'Are we beginning to commend ourselves again?' (2 Corinthians 3:1a).

Jesus came into the world as Saviour and suffering servant, all grace and truth, a shining light both to the Jews and the Gentiles. He was crucified and buried, but then rose from the dead, to be in heaven where he reigns today, waiting for the time to return in glory. Now, all Christians are meant to be 'reflectors' of the light of Christ in a spiritually darkening world, as we await the Lord's return.

In the 'explosion' of the incarnation (the moment of Jesus' birth) we see the action of God, who plunged into our world, and lives—and is to be discovered alive—among us. Jesus dwells in those who receive him; he comes to occupy us for the display of his divine splendour. We become a 'temple' of the Holy Spirit. Too often, though, some Christians are tempted to speak as if they somehow *own* a little of God. Our common mistake in evangelism is to give the impression that we are actually saying, 'Without what I have, you are poor and ignorant—not to mention lost, and probably damned! I am the proprietor of what you need to receive.' Have we fallen into the trap of believing that we *own*, or *possess* God, or his power? To put it slightly differently, do we think we 'have' God, when really it is he who has us? We can *receive* the Holy Spirit, yet the Holy Spirit does not, thereby, become our 'possession'. Yes, God is faithful to his covenant promises, and when we pray according to his word he is faithful to his own self-revelation. He honours the faithfulness of his people. But he is Lord; he is sovereign; and our part is to remain in a position of humility and faith, confident that he will do as he has said. It is a matter of having the right perspective; and a right understanding of this matter is extremely important, for it affects our relationship with God and our relationships with others in a very deep way. St. Paul explained very clearly what our attitude should be. '...Since we have such a hope, we are very bold' (2 Corinthians 3:12). That is as it should be. But that proper boldness in passing on the good news of Jesus Christ must be matched by humility and love, not self-centredness for, as Paul goes on to say: '...we have this treasure in jars of clay to show that this all-surpassing power is from God and not from us' (2 Corinthians 4:7).

To shine with the light of Jesus, then, is not a matter of deliberately projecting something we 'possess', as though we were the proprietors of a piece of property, but, rather, allowing the Holy Spirit to use us, to bear fruit in us—fruit that he will grow in us as we walk closely with Jesus in obedience, and continually praise and worship him. In this way, we hope to become more transparent to his light, which can shine through us. At the heart of this is the desire to be in the Lord's presence continually:

THE TELEVISION STUDIO

> One thing I ask of the LORD,
> this is what I seek:
> that I may dwell in the house of the LORD
> all the days of my life,
> to gaze upon the beauty of the LORD
> and to seek him in his temple.
>
> *Psalm 27:4*

The psalmist expresses a great longing to be in constant communion with the Lord, in his temple, the place of worship. When the Holy Spirit comes, we are amazingly privileged to *be* his temple, but he remains sovereign; he is to be in control, and when we minister to others, we do so under *his* authority, according to *his* word, and at *his* prompting.

The time for reflecting and waiting was over. In the studio, the final call came. Off we set, along the winding television studio corridors, with our hearts in our throats. As we took our places, me on my chair and Yates on his plinth, a lady appeared out of nowhere. "Hi, I'm Gillian! Soft and gentle, soft and gentle!" she sang at me. I did not know quite what to say to this approach, and Yates kept silent, too. Then, to my male horror, she produced a powder puff and began to dab my face with it. First one side and then the other, across the forehead and up under the hairline. As she was finishing, a black head barged into the back of my shoulder, and Yates let loose the smallest and most gentle of moans in his throat. It sounded something like, "Don't you let that woman near me!" I had to agree with him.

FIND THE WAY!

Yates grizzled again. "She's not taking the shine off me!" Happily, she did not.

The audience was ushered in and the filming went off with a swing. Yates and I both shone in our differing ways. His glossy coat rippled and sparkled in the studio lights while he posed for the cameras, and I grappled with the questions, one of which was quite a triumph for a blind man. "On your monitors," said the question master, "is a photograph of a building. Which building is it?" I had been told by the producer to lower my head towards the monitor whenever a visual question came up, and this I did, finding my team captain leaning towards me.

He whispered in my ear, "It's a church. Wait a moment, there's a bloke in the foreground wearing an Arab sort of head-dress—I bet it's in the Middle East." We paused to reflect, as neither of us had been to Israel, the most likely location, we thought.

"Have you any idea at all?" asked my team captain, through the side of his mouth. I mumbled something back about the Church of the Holy Sepulchre, because it was the only one in that region I had ever heard of and could remember at that moment.

"Mike has the answer!" My captain raised his hands in loud triumph. "What is it, Mike?"

"The Church of the Holy Sepulchre", I offered.

"Absolutely right!" shouted the question master. "Four points to Mike's team!"

'How wonderful,' I thought. The only question I solved on my own was a visual one! Yates must have been very proud of me. An hour later, and with some rejoicing, we were back out in the sunshine, holding our heads high, as winners do!

6

Heads in the Sand

*Trust in the LORD with all your heart
and lean not on your own understanding;
in all your ways acknowledge him,
and he will make your paths straight.*

Proverbs 3:5–6

As we have already noticed, Yates does not like the rain. Puddles are sometimes acceptable, rivers and lakes are a huge blessing, but rain, for some reason known only to him, is completely oppressive. He hates it.

There is, however, a wonderful thing about rain—it is heavenly to get away from! Arriving at work soaked through to the skin may seem like the end of the road, but Yates' tail rises up with expectation. He knows that indoors, hanging on a peg over a radiator, is his towel. At the sight of it being held out before him by whoever is acting in the role of 'towelmaster', he starts to lose control of his usually placid (and somewhat superior) temperament. His whole body begins to waggle and shake from nose to tail. As the towel is wrapped around his body and the rubbing begins, the ecstasy level increases beyond anything a dog could ever reasonably be expected to bear. Down goes his head into the carpet, and up comes his bottom, tail thrashing from side to side with the thrill of having his back rubbed. At this point, most 'towelmasters' are reduced to fits of giggles at his obvious enjoyment of the treatment. They cannot resist continuing. Yates then tries to bury deeper — first one side of the head and then the other is pushed into the carpet at the 'towelmaster's' feet. Squirming and grunting with delight, Yates tingles with the rapture of the rub.

Does Yates coolly calculate that the more he displays his natural rapture in this way, the greater the effort that will be made by the 'towelmaster'? Who knows.... But, if that is so, there would be a similarity with the way some of us behave! There is, in quite a few folk, a tendency to manipulate, in order to get the attention we feel we need.

Sometimes, we all encounter people who are 'trapped' in a certain kind of behaviour pattern that has not done anything for them in the past, yet is continually repeated. In the cases of some, who are desperately longing to be loved, their minds seem to be telling them that if they behave in a needy, vulnerable way, then perhaps others will take pity on them and give love. That approach never 'works' in reality. Others do not give the sort of affirmation they desire. It may always work for guide dogs who want the 'towel treatment', but it is a futile, self-destructive pattern for us. How I long for people to find release from this 'imprisonment' in a tragic misunderstanding, and to find true freedom in assurance of the Lord's personal love.

When I remember back to the early beginnings of

losing my sight, thirty years or so ago, I have some empathy for those who express need and vulnerability as a means of seeking love. I tried the same tactic. It did not work for me, either! It took me a while to realise that this way of behaving is not terribly productive. Eventually, I gave up the pattern and found another model that works better for everyone, and is much more in line with the teaching and example of Jesus: to stop *searching* for love and start *giving* it, instead.

This has proved to be considerably more successful and much healthier. I can still slip into a feeling of being needy and vulnerable on rare occasions, but I know, nowadays, that this is a fruitless way of trying to persuade people to love me. In truth, it seems to have the opposite effect. It actually drives people away! When someone fails to learn and put into practice this important lesson, the same old pattern of seeking to manipulate others so that they will, it is hoped, deliver what is wanted, just goes on and on, until those who live around the 'manipulator', whether in church or at home, start to feel, not pity and affection, but something more like exasperation. But on we go, so often making the same old errors over and over again. It was once put to me that it is almost as though we seem to drive around and around the one-way system, always hitting the same pothole. We seem to do this in the hope that, next time around, the hole in the road will have spontaneously disappeared—but it never does.

So how can people be released from the emotional 'hard work' of seeking to control and manipulate others into giving affection and love? Above all, they need to be assured of the 'blanket warmth' of God's personal love; really discovering in experience, not just in theory, that this is truly sufficient for their needs. Giving real assent to the gospel of Jesus Christ, receiving him as Lord and Saviour in a personal way, and then going on being filled with the Holy Spirit, takes our eyes off our own small self-justifying patch of reality. In that living relationship, we begin to discover for ourselves that we are loved, and that our true citizenship is in heaven. The battle against old ways of thinking and relating must still be fought, but first of all our confidence must be in Jesus. We may be looking to others to provide what only he can really provide. We may also be looking to religious effort to sustain our sense of self-worth and, unsurprisingly, we find that this is just not effective.

If you know people who are caught in the sort of trap we have been considering, pray for them, that they may truly know the liberty that Jesus wills and can bring about for them. He wants to release them from the pain that is at the heart of their pattern of behaviour. It is for *freedom* that Christ has set us free. The work of the Holy Spirit is crucial in this, as we fight on the 'battleground' of the mind against wrong understandings of who we are and how we should relate to others. For our part, we need to ask the Lord to show us any ways in which we are seeking to 'manipulate' others' emotions, repent of any such sinful attitudes, and remind ourselves again that we have received 'the spirit of sonship' which is the Lord's gift to Christians, and we have to live in awareness of it; we are not to dominate, control and manipulate others, but to know that he loves us. Jesus is Lord, and we are safe with him—forever. He alone can assure us of our worth and so provide the ultimate security; his word stands for ever, and we are to learn to depend upon *his* wonderful promises and *his* abiding presence.

7

Loneliness

A father to the fatherless, a defender of widows,
is God in his holy dwelling.
God sets the lonely in families,
he leads forth the prisoners with singing;
but the rebellious live in a sun-scorched land.

Psalm 68:5–6

It was hot; quite hot enough to make a black guide dog fairly miserable. The problem was that Yates' skin pigment and hair soaked up the heat, so no amount of drinking and panting brought relief. Yates sought out shade in the garden wherever he could find it, and was most relieved to go away with me to a Christian conference in mid Wales —relieved because conferences mean being indoors and out of the glare of the sun, for long periods of time. There would be an extra bonus there—plenty of opportunity for snoozing on the platform while Dad goes on and on and on....

FIND THE WAY!

We were pleased to arrive at the venue and cool off in the big, airy arenas, with all the doors open to catch the welcome draughts. Half way through the week, I noticed that Yates' tail was not performing as usual. Normally, it does not stop moving, but then it hung, uselessly, like a limp flag on a still day.

As we strolled around the conference site, we were greeted with all the customary cries of, "Hi Yates!" —but there was no response. Usually, such a shout would bring his tail up high and swinging, but nothing happened. Whatever was going on, he was suffering alone.

For three days I had simply assumed that the heat had put him 'under the weather' and that all would be well again as soon as we got home. But there was little sign of his getting any better. Even more worrying was the little cry he gave, every time I spoke his name myself, and it took another day for me to see what was happening. His joy at having his name called by his master was pressing the tail into service, and the corresponding yelp of pain was the tail refusing to comply. Something had gone very wrong. Friends had a look, but could see nothing. One or two prayed for him. He must have felt very lonely, locked up with his pain, and not being able to explain it.

I fell to thinking very deeply about this whole question of loneliness, as we human beings experience it. It is a condition that can be extremely miserable. Yet it can be difficult to help the lonely without trotting out what sound awfully like 'pat' statements —even those comments which are intended to sound Christian may not be timely, and may be received by the lonely person as mere 'jargon'. Somehow, the reality of what is being felt has to be acknowledged. Moreover, what is really needed may be just to know that someone is there who cares. Loneliness itself is a terrible thing, and so many people, young and old, suffer from it.

Our society encourages us to nurture the art of being happy alone, but this is often impossible. There are so many different types of loneliness, and when we have conquered one or two of them others can appear.

The hunger pains of loneliness, experienced by the elderly especially, are often very acute. The long-term unemployed, the homeless, those who have voluntarily left home, or even country, to find work or an education, these people can also be numbered among the lonely especially during holiday times, traditional religious seasons and times of family celebration.

Those of us who are blessed in being surrounded by our loved-ones may readily (and wrongly) assume that loneliness arises from being separated somehow from people. We can be completely surrounded by a mass of humanity, yet still be lonely. We may simply be lacking like-minded fellowship or any particular depth of friendship. It would not be unusual in many cities and on many housing estates to spend years surrounded by thousands of people. We might see hundreds every day, yet make only a single friend. It quite often seems that the larger the city, the greater the loneliness to be found there. Elderly people living on their own with only infrequent visits from friends and relatives are particularly vulnerable to the dragging heartache of loneliness. To make it worse, those who are not able to enjoy physical activity have time on their hands to sit and contemplate alone the joys and noise of family life now past.

In all these cases, we need to help the lonely to find the indestructible relationship that comes from a close walk with the Lord. As a friend of Jesus, one truly is never alone. Knowing the Fatherhood of God, we are assured of the love of one who will never let us down. With the indwelling, anointing Holy Spirit, we have life rather than emptiness. All this blessing is available, and when we taste for ourselves the goodness of God's presence, our solitude is no longer the horrible loneliness it used to be, for we know *from experience*, not merely words, that we really are not alone. Even in the valleys we have a cure for loneliness, as we remember the words about God that Moses spoke to the Israelite people:

> "The LORD himself goes before you and will be with you; he will never leave you nor forsake you; Do not be afraid; do not be discouraged."
>
> *Deuteronomy 31:8*

To help the lonely to get in touch with all that God has for them (and for us) is one of the best ways we can minister to them.

What an encouragement, too, to know that God has entered into the reality of human aloneness. How alone Jesus was on Good Friday, as the crowds watched his dying; and how desolate were his disciples later that same day —surrounded by people, yet still so desperately alone.

There is another kind of aloneness, which can be experienced by those with a particular calling from God, accepted as part of their vocation. Think of the solitude of John the Baptist, during his time in the wilderness. The baptising prophet lived in the desert, between the centre of Judaea and the Dead Sea. One of the most terrible deserts in the world, it is a limestone wilderness, warped and twisted. The rock shimmers in the blisteringly hot haze of the daytime heat, and it sounds hollow to the feet, as though there were a vast furnace underneath. It stretches to the Dead Sea, descending in dreadful, unclimbable cliff faces down to sea level. In this cheerless, barren, lonely spot, John spent time communing with God. What we do not know, of course, is whether John experienced in that solitude the pain of loneliness. We may properly suppose that God sustained him, as he obediently did what he was shown he had to do.

The lesson that we might learn from John the Baptist may be constructive in our own times and places of solitude. It may be that sometimes our lives need stripping of all the clutter of the years, so that we can get down to basics. We need a personal relationship with the Lord Jesus Christ to be whole human beings. We need to know him as Lord and Saviour.

Was that time of solitude necessary for John, so that he would better know both himself and the will of God? We need to know *ourselves*, too—what goes on inside us—and this often cannot happen until we have got rid of whatever is clogging up our spiritual life. Those times of solitude that we experience as loneliness may be, spiritually, very beneficial, if used positively —part of that 'unclogging' process. There may not, however, be a great deal we can accomplish in overcoming our neighbour's loneliness if we are in a state of being hard-pressed to cope with our own.

At the conference I had been trying to offer friendly, Christian comfort to Yates in his lonely trial but, in some way beyond my understanding, he was on the lookout, too.

FIND THE WAY!

One evening, we set off, as usual, from our room to the main arena, for the evening celebration service. Yates knew the ropes very well by now—straight in through the right-hand entrance door, and across to the blocks of seating. On each evening of that conference, he had taken the same route. We turned right at the chairs, walked sedately down the far right-hand aisle between the seating and the window wall, turned left at the end, and across the front row of seats to the centre aisle. At this point we would find an empty seat for me, and Yates would have all the room in the world to stretch out and sleep through the entire proceedings.

Not tonight! Instead of turning right towards the front of the arena, Yates swung left, heading for the back. I long ago learned to go with the flow when he does anything unusual—he is so in control of situations that it is always best to assume that he knows best. We passed alongside the ends of some twenty or so rows, until we found a gangway between them. With no command from me, he headed off down this cross-aisle until he reached the far side of the building, turned sharply to his right and marched purposefully down towards the front.

About half way along this last passage, he stopped because of four or five ladies standing in the way. They had their backs to us, and were deep in joyous conversation about something or other—completely unaware that we were waiting to pass. Eventually, I coughed loudly and apologised, urging Yates to go forward as they parted to let us through. The dog would not move. There was plenty of space to get through, but all four anchors were firmly embedded in the carpet. No matter what urging and encouraging commands I used, he would not budge an inch.

LONELINESS

"I'm so sorry about this!" I offered, getting very embarrassed at Yates' lack of obedience.

"That's alright," said one of the ladies. "Please don't worry about it. You see, I'm very used to dealing with dogs —I'm a vet!" Immediately, I told her about the tail problem, and she took Yates off somewhere to have a calm and private look at him. She diagnosed a bruised tail— perhaps a child had pulled it or someone had trodden on it.

What an extraordinary dog! How had he managed that? How did he know that he should find a vet? How did he know what they look like? How did he know where to find one?

God is gracious enough to answer so many different kinds of prayer, in so many different ways!

8

Slippery Character

Do nothing out of selfish ambition or vain conceit, but in humility consider others better than yourselves. Each of you should look not only to your own interests, but also to the interests of others.
Philippians 2:3–4

Look to the interests of others? How different this is from the way that the world views life! Everything seems to be trying to persuade us that we need to look out for number one; that it is a 'dog eat dog' world (sorry, Yates!), and that the only thing which really matters in the end is getting to the top of whatever particular pile we have been dumped on by life. If we have to step on a few people along the way, well, that is tough, and no one should be surprised. After all, whoever has the most toys wins!

Whoever has the most toys? It was after Easter, and after lunch, and the perfect afternoon for lounging in a comfortable armchair, glass of wine in one hand and dog lead in the other, listening to a friend play his guitar, while wondering what the summer would hold for us. My hosts had two black Labradors of their own, who kept a respectful distance from the mighty Yates as he lay on the carpet at my feet, self-crowned king of all he surveyed.

Well, I suppose that is the characteristic of being a natural pack leader—things which are surveyed are 'possessed'. To see is to own, even if continuous possession and re-possession of other people's belongings is a constant embarrassment to this particular self-appointed dictator's owner! Now, he was about to do it again. After the most pleasant hour in the company of good Christian friends, my host's wife, Jacqui, kindly suggested, "Shall I take all the dogs out for a walk, as they seem to get on so well together?"

Yates stood up, stretched out his front paws and lowered his chest to the floor, yawned and turned to face the door. "What's everyone waiting for?"

They were gone for a while, running, sniffing and generally being three dogs together in the large garden. After a further half hour, I heard the front door slam shut, and a shriek from Jacqui: "Oh no! My slippers!" On leaving the house, she had left them in the corner of the hall, for her return. Yates had walked sedately in through the front door and across the hall, lifted one slipper, and was strolling towards the door to the sitting room and Dad. One of the pursuing house dogs cottoned on to the idea and collected up the other slipper. But wait a moment! What is seen is possessed! The top dog has all the toys! Yates froze. Without moving his body, he turned his head to glare at this upstart of a dog, who had dared to lift a slipper—one of *his* slippers at that. The word 'growl' may be too strong. A short and low rumble of corrective warning set up in Yates' throat, and the desired effect was instantly achieved. Our host's dog stopped dead in its tracks, dropped our hostess's slipper, and wandered away to find his owner. Then Yates turned, laid his slipper down beside the other, picked up both, and came back to lie at my feet. There is no doubt about it—Yates owns everything!

God challenges us to look at life in a very different way from that. We are to care for the welfare of others, and to look out for their interests with as much diligence as we look out for our own. Scripture asks us to lay aside our empty ambitions and selfish conceits, regarding ourselves with a good deal of humility. We Christians are called to let go of our natural human need to be first, to be better at most things than other people, and begin to let the interests of those around us take precedence from time to time.

This is not easy, but is the point at which we can begin to experience real Christian growth, learning the joy of giving, and experiencing the peace that comes from it in return. Driving to work, we need to let those pushy drivers get onto the main road in front of us —and smile at them, not grumble. We can stop for the woman who wants to use the crossing; another thirty seconds or so will not make a great deal of difference to the morning, and we will have shown consideration. When we are waiting in the local supermarket queue, we could try letting someone into the line ahead of us—this not only surprises them and lightens their day, but brightens ours as well! There are so many ways we can bless others in word and deed, putting their interests first.

Our Lord Jesus laid aside his position and power,

looking out for *our* interests, showing us the true nature of love as he did so. He came both as Saviour and suffering servant —dying for our sins, that we might live and know his glory.

How we all need to lay aside the selfish ambition and conceit that hamper us from becoming more like Jesus, the Son of God; looking out for the interests of others, encouraging them with a kind word or a smile whenever we can!

9

The Harvester

Jesus went through all the towns and villages, teaching in their synagogues, preaching the good news of the kingdom and healing every disease and sickness. When he saw the crowds, he had compassion on them, because they were harassed and helpless, like sheep without a shepherd. Then he said to his disciples, "The harvest is plentiful but the workers are few. Ask the Lord of the harvest, therefore, to send out workers into his harvest field."

Matthew 9:35,38

It has always seemed to me to be a little strange that dogs should enjoy fruit. I can readily associate them with bones, biscuits, chocolate and dog meal —but soft fruit? Our previous pet spaniel, Katie, had a taste for harvesting, which was discovered too late. In those far-off days, we grew strawberries on a small plot at the bottom of the vegetable garden, but with little success. Other fruits were always to be had in abundance, but not strawberries. The abundance of God's fruitfulness swelled all around the garden above knee height, but never below. One evening in high summer, while we were strolling round the garden, a snuffling and rustling noise came from the direction of the strawberry netting. Pressed in underneath the anti-devouring bird net cover was a spaniel, flat on her stomach, harvesting. No wonder we never had any strawberries!

Yates is different. He is much taken by grapes —the unfermented variety, I should add. In fact, he has a tendency to swallow them whole. This seems to negate the whole purpose of eating them; one would have thought that they would taste best when bitten through, so that the juices flow. Before Yates came to live with us, we had a vine growing in an old, wooden greenhouse. This structure was eventually dismantled, because of its state of brokenness, incidentally. Perhaps this is just as well —or we might never have been able to harvest any grapes, either!

Jesus spoke vividly about the work of harvesting. His words are so powerful:

> "Listen to another parable: There was a landowner who planted a vineyard. He put a wall around it, dug a winepress in it and built a watchtower. Then he rented the vineyard to some farmers and went away on a journey. When the harvest time approached, he sent his servants to the tenants to collect his fruit.
>
> "The tenants seized his servants; they beat one, killed another, and stoned a third. Then he sent other servants to them, more than the first time, and the tenants treated them in the same way. Last of all, he sent his son to them. 'They will respect my son,' he said.
>
> "But when the tenants saw the son, they said to each

other, 'This is the heir. Come, let's kill him and take his inheritance.' So they took him and threw him out of the vineyard and killed him...."

Matthew 21:33–39

This parable probably tells us more than any other about Jesus—who he is and why he came to live among us. It tells the story of Good Friday before it happened. It also reminds us that God is the true owner of the vineyard. Although we might well own our homes, such tenure is only a matter of human and legal convenience. God is the true 'landlord' of this world and we are the tenants.

The harvest God wants from this world, his vineyard, is still the same fruit —souls, not grapes! The harvest is plentiful, but, as Jesus pointed out, the workers are few. In the early church period, it took many years of hard toil and foot-slogging to take God's message to what was, to the first Christians, the known world. Today, the 'vineyard' is the whole planet. We can cross this 'vineyard' from one end to the other, by plane, in the space of twenty-four hours. Almost every corner of it can be reached by satellite television, radio, the press, and various forms of telecommunications. Yet the task of Christians is still essentially the same as that of those people to whom Jesus directed the parable of the tenants, and those wonderfully determined early evangelists and witnesses who spread the good news of Jesus Christ around their world. What has changed? —our ability to harvest that vineyard. Because of advances in technology of all kinds, we now have better opportunities than ever before to carry out, in our own age, the great commission —to preach that the kingdom of heaven is near, heal the sick, raise the dead, cleanse those who have leprosy, and drive out demons.

There remains, however, the question of our personal resolve to bring in the harvest. We actually have to carry out the task! Persistence, a refusal to be deflected or give up, an urge to try, try and try again is needed, in order to gather in the harvest. It is easy to fall into one of two camps when confronted with any demanding task or challenge. There are those who say, 'It's hopeless', and there are those who say, 'I'll try.' Over and over again, in the stories of the healing miracles of Jesus, it was the man or woman who was prepared to press forward and try who received the healing. The people who lowered a paralysed man into the room through a hole in the roof, bringing him to Jesus' feet; the man with the withered hand; the man with leprosy, and many others, witness to our need for faith, determination and appropriate action in these things. God wants us to try, to make an effort, so that others may be powerfully blessed by our witness.

'I must do something' will always solve more problems in the world than 'something ought to be done'. Saying 'yes' to being a harvester for the kingdom of God means 'rolled-up sleeves' and both hands being plunged into life —up to the elbows! Ordinary people who find themselves falling in with God's plan become extraordinary in a particular way. They have taken hold of the promises of God, and they exercise faith in and by their actions. Their hope is securely placed in Jesus; and their faith is, indeed, the 'substance of things hoped for'. The apostles were ordinary men who became extraordinary because they placed themselves in the flow of God's purposes, in the power of the Holy Spirit. They became a part of Christ's mission in the world; and any one of us, by the grace of God, can do the same.

In the kingdom of God, God sets the goals! He is King in the kingdom. His command is given in the great commission. (See Matthew 28:19–20). The key task is making disciples in all nations. He gives us the desire to witness to Jesus in many different settings. We are led by the Holy Spirit, and his direction can come in many ways, and might include dreams, visions and prophetic words, all duly confirmed and tested on biblical principles. Every Christian, without exception, is called to be a faithful, persistent, diligent witness in the kingdom. Can *we* change the world? Not in our *own* strength, of course; yet God can use us to bring about changes that will be far beyond what we imagine. He gives his servants authority to offer his transforming, scriptural word to anyone we can reach out and touch with the love of Jesus; and the Holy Spirit is always ready to fill us, empower us and equip us for this great task. If we have helped someone along life's path, in the name of Jesus; if we have encouraged anyone; if someone is closer to Jesus now because of the things that, by the grace of God, we may have been led to say or do, or pray —then we have been privileged to help with the most important harvest of all: the fulfilment of that great commission. This is not just for the harvester's own satisfaction; but we will, indeed, taste the sweetness of seeing precious souls find salvation, healing, freedom from bondage and beginning to experience abundant life, as they respond to the word of God, come to Jesus, receive him and begin to enjoy all the benefits he won for them and us, by the shedding of his precious blood on the cross. We share the rejoicing of heaven as this harvest is gathered in.

10

Pastimes

*Do not fret because of evil men
or be envious of those who do wrong;
for like the grass they will soon wither,
like green plants they will soon die away.
Trust in the LORD and do good;
dwell in the land and enjoy safe pasture.
Delight yourself in the LORD
and he will give you the desires of your heart.
Commit your way to the LORD;
trust in him and he will do this:*

Psalm 37:1–5

Like any serious, adult, self-respecting, highly trained and professional working dog, Yates plays games. He entertains himself. I suppose it is all to do with some sort of off-duty, letting hair down; although there are times I do not bless the volume of dog hair that does come down!

Pride of place among all his toys is the football. There are tennis balls and rubber pulls, sticks and clothes pegs but all are as nothing, compared with the joys of the football.

Yates is also the proud possessor of nine tennis balls, but these do not carry the same attraction for him. This may be an outworking of his own guilt, as they have all been scooped up, at breakneck speed, from the somewhat overgrown edges of a local public tennis court, mostly while play was still in progress!

His football, however, is not a full-size, correctly inflated bladder, fit to grace a professional soccer stadium, but a sad, soggy and deflated, but much adored, sack of decomposing leather, with a hole in it. Why is it so entertaining? It makes noises. The hole in it is the right size to allow a hiss—almost a whistle—to issue from its insides, every time the mighty black jaws are clamped around its girth. Not only can this chomping and chewing provide endless moments of pleasure on the lawn, but, hopefully, the sound of this exhaling ball can be used to tease and goad passers-by into 'let's chase' mode. This effect is often produced by shoving the hissing ball into the back of a passing knee or, and this is even greater sport, pressing the ball down on the foot of a seated admirer, knowing full well that feet cannot grip it, and are therefore quite safe to tease!

At least it is all honest, innocent entertainment, which is more than can be said for the ways many human beings today keep themselves occupied. Has that not always been a matter of concern for all who are concerned with godliness? It would have been around AD 64 that Paul was sufficiently concerned about local pastimes to remind Roman Christians of the need for strength to resist the goings-on of his day.

Furthermore, since they did not think it worth while to retain the knowledge of God, he gave them over to a depraved mind, to do what ought not to be done. They have become filled with every kind of wickedness, evil, greed and depravity. They are full of envy, murder, strife, deceit and malice. They are gossips, slanderers, God-haters, insolent, arrogant and boastful; they invent ways of doing evil; they disobey their parents; they are senseless, faithless, heartless, ruthless.

Romans 1:28–31

Nothing seems to have changed, except that there are, nowadays, vastly more opportunities to stray from the true path, in the name of 'entertainment'. Once it was reading, fishing and walks in the country; now it is pornography, drugs and ever more violent crime. Television, which blossomed with such a fanfare about educational excellence in the fifties, is seen by many to have degenerated into being a vehicle for the display of violence and depravity. Even family shows depict the breaking up of marriages as being something 'natural' and 'acceptable', and divorce as being almost inevitable; de facto relationships are now called 'partnerships'.

There is nothing new about any of this. The Roman Empire, about which Paul was writing, had entertainment of an even more violent nature, which appealed to many of its citizens. Why does such degradation occur?

The Bible declares that, '...the whole world is a prisoner of sin, so that what was promised, being given through faith in Jesus Christ, might be given to those who believe' (Galatians 3:22). I have become convinced that no one is permanently contented in sinful pursuits. They can have no real peace. My counselling experience shows me a disturbed state of mind in people who have embraced sinful patterns of behaviour. Sometimes, the road to freedom in Jesus Christ begins for them as they see a righteous model in good Christians, and start to acknowledge their sin for what it is. The Spirit leads them to repentance and faith, as they perceive their need and come to the cross for forgiveness and new life.

What stance are we to adopt in the face of sin and evil in the world around us? Sometimes, especially when there is too much going on around me in this busy, crazy world, I feel it is sensible, safe and secure, just to rest in the knowledge that my priorities are firmly set. Let us remind ourselves again of four key priorities, which should govern our pattern of behaviour and attitude, and which in time transform the way we deal with the world around us.

At the heart of it all there is our relationship with God: that relationship is the most important thing in life, and is to govern all our other priorities. When Martha was cleaning and Mary was listening to Jesus, Martha tried to persuade her to help with the work. Jesus told her,

> "...but only one thing is needed. Mary has chosen what is better, and it will not be taken away from her."
>
> *Luke 10:42*

The main concern for our lives has to be learning from Jesus, sitting at his feet, worshipping him, spending time with him. Do you make that your top priority?

Then there is the matter of having the right attitude to

life. How tempting it is to dwell on past failures (our own and those of others), but, as Paul reminds us, the Christian approach is to be forward looking.

> But one thing I do: Forgetting what is behind and straining towards what is ahead, I press on towards the goal to win the prize for which God has called me heavenwards in Christ Jesus.
> *Philippians 3:13b–14*

We have to find a way to let go of the past, including our hurts, 'the way we have always done it', our own sin and guilt, and all bitterness and resentment; or such things colour our responses and create barriers to enjoying a right relationship with the Lord, and the abundant life he wills for us. Sometimes, when I have found it hard to be free from a particular sin or sense of guilt, I have written that sin down on a piece of paper, folded it up, set it alight and, after repenting, recited Hebrews 8:12 —

> "For I will forgive their wickedness and will remember their sins no more."

When I have brought my sin to the cross and repented of it, God no longer remembers it. So my task is to receive, and be aware of, that amazing divine forgiveness which is given only through the blood of Jesus.

Thirdly, we need to recall that the only sort of *deed* that counts is faith expressing itself through love. Faith is trust in God that manifests itself in a willingness to act, even when I do not understand. Love includes caring about the real needs and feelings of others. What really matters is a trust in God which reveals itself in our caring about other people.

Fourthly, we need to know where our true security lies. Building our security and our life on anything in this world will, at some point, bring inevitable feelings of insecurity because nothing is unshakeable. None of the activities, even good activities, that the world offers, can provide us with true inner peace and security. A sense of insecurity can make any of us extremely unhappy. Most people try to find security in things that are inherently insecure: relationships, money and possessions.

God is eternal. Finding our security in him alone is fundamental to finding a solid life. The most important thing in life is our relationship with God the Father through Jesus Christ, and it shows in our concerns, our actions, our attitudes and our assurance concerning our final destination, our sense that our true citizenship is in heaven, for, as the Bible says,

> ...you are a chosen people, a royal priesthood, a holy nation, a people belonging to God, that you may declare the praises of him who called you out of darkness into his wonderful light.
>
> *1 Peter 2:9*

The sound and movement of Yates playing serves as my constant reminder to enjoy life as it has been given to me. The deceits, entertainments and diversions of this life are not to be (or to govern) our goals and priorities. Nor will they ever provide peace, security and true joy. The real sin of the world is to put man and his pleasures at the centre. True faith acknowledges the kingship of God, and puts *his* revealed will and purposes at the centre, rather than our own or the world's purposes and pleasures.

God longs for us to seek him; when we seek him, according to his promise, he allows us to find him; and when we have found him, his Holy Spirit leads us to obey him. Everything else flows from this.

11

Control

Be shepherds of God's flock that is under your care, serving as overseers—not because you must, but because you are willing, as God wants you to be; not greedy for money, but eager to serve; not lording it over those entrusted to you, but being examples to the flock.

1 Peter 5:2–3

I suppose there will always be pack leaders in any grouping in our society: human or animal. Yates is, most definitely, a pack leader.

From time to time during my initial four week training period away from home, learning to handle my new guide dog, we would go for a walk on the local racecourse. Naturally there were no horses, just ten dogs from the training school, charging up and down, stretching their legs and enjoying their freedom.

The racecourse was purpose-built for these occasions. The track is easily wide enough for ten wanna-be guide dog owners to link arms, along with two or three trainers, and wander round the course in small groups or in line abreast behind the dogs.

One of the four legged fun-hunters stood out above the rest, however. Yates would disappear off on his own into the bushes and hedges along the side of the track, snuffling about until he came up with a suitable object for the chase! The most practical toy for this purpose was an empty, discarded, plastic, soft drink bottle. Yates emerged from the undergrowth to dance and prance in front of the attending tribe of Labradors and students, offering aloft his prized possession and tempting the dogs to follow him in the chase wherever he decided to go. This was certainly crowd manipulation, but of a harmless kind.

That passage in I Peter has something to say to leaders who, rather than shepherding their flock, rebuke them into submission and, like the Pharisees, know the letter of the law, but not the spirit. Unhappily, such leaders do exist in church, business, education and other walks of life. Some use false threats, or guilt, to control those around them; others use various forms of legalism. When the early church slipped back into legalism, Paul asked, "Who has bewitched you?" (Galatians 3:1b.) Control can be a 'devilish' thing. People who have a *need* to control others, whether in the church or more usually elsewhere, are themselves insecure and immature. Only when they feel that they are in a position to manipulate those under or around them do they gain a false sense of security. Whilst this need to control is an emotional sickness, it has spiritual and emotional effects on those they control, and can be psychologically damaging to them as well.

On top of all this, both secular and church leaders who

control others are usurping the position that should be occupied by God in the lives of those they manipulate.

However, there is another side to this evil coin. When we allow ourselves to be controlled by other people, becoming dependent on them to tell us what we should or should not do, instead of yielding to the directing of God's Spirit, we behave like children needing a parent figure for our own security. In doing this, we become involved in our controller's sickness, because of our own insecurity and lack of wisdom! We do not have to think for ourselves, nor to accept responsibility for our decisions and, what is more, we can then blame someone else for our bad choices.

Whilst we do not have the ability to change others, we most certainly can change ourselves, with God's help, by not allowing others to control us or lord it over us! That is our own responsibility.

Co-dependency in controlling relationships comes in many differing shapes and sizes but, at bottom, it is doing for others what they can do and need to do for themselves. It may make the person we are helping ('enabling') feel good for the time being, and it may make the 'enabler' feel important and wanted, but it keeps both of them over-dependent on each other. It usually does not help either of them in the long run.

Another common aspect of control is the need to 'rescue' people from their problems. This, too, may keep them over-dependent on us and, as long as we go on taking their responsibilities from them, they have no need to get well or resolve their problems, with or without God's help, and to recover. A friend, who was born with no hearing, and with tiny hands protruding from the shoulder blades, remembers that, when he was only four or five years old, he found it very difficult to pull a shirt over his head and shoulders. On one of these 'struggling occasions', a family friend said to his watching mother, "Why don't you help him?" To which she replied, "I am."

It may not have seemed like it to him at the time, but that was real—albeit tough—love.

On those occasions when we do anything for someone else that they could have, should have, and needed to do for themselves, we are not actually helping them, nor even doing the loving thing for them. We may be keeping them over-dependent on us. It may make both parties feel good at the time, but in the long run we are hurting them.

The awful bottom line of co-dependency, especially between controlling leaders and weak followers, is that *need* is mistaken for *love*. The co-dependent needs others to need him in order to make him feel good about himself. What we do may look like love, and it may look very Christian, but it is neither. The co-dependent is doing what he is doing for himself —always! His motive is off-balance.

God will 'bend the heavens' to help us when we cannot help ourselves—that is why he sent Jesus to die for our sins—but he will not do for us what we can and need to do for ourselves. He has promised to give us wisdom and direction if we ask for it, and courage if we need that as well. Once we know what we need to do in any given situation, it is up to us to 'trust and obey' —and just do it!

The interesting question about the racecourse scene with Yates is this: who was really in control? Yates was certainly demonstrating manipulative control in his 'born to be a pack leader' sort of way, but would he come straight to me when I blew his whistle? That was part of his training —returning to heel at the sound of three good toots. Well, that is the theory, anyway, and this time it worked —back he came!

12

Devious Devices

For we are not unaware of his [Satan's] schemes.
II Corinthians 2:11b

The patio got built —in the end. As the last days of spring approached, I telephoned the builders every week, increasingly desperate to make sure that they started on time and finished the project before the summer arrived. I was longing for two or three hot days of doing as little as possible other than listening to the cricket on the radio, and snoozing in the sun.

In the end, I need not have worried so much—there was about a week's fine weather after project completion day, but then it rained off and on for weeks afterwards!

It took about two weeks to build the mighty edifice of railway sleepers, impacted rubble and cut flagstones, with clematis trellis all the way around. The workforce varied from day to day between one and four hard-working young men; but always there was one guide dog in attendance, on the look-out!

Yates awarded himself the role of 'clean-up person'.

FIND THE WAY!

The building site, he decided, would have to be kept spick and span. He moved in like greased lightening every time a gardening glove was dropped, and caught every crisp packet before it floated to the ground. Day after day, he removed pliers and bags of nails from the site and re-stacked all the timber off-cuts, in a looser, more distributive manner, around the garden. He worked as hard as any of them!

A few days before the project neared completion, I heard a scream from the garden, and rushed out through the back door to investigate. Had someone been hurt?

"What's the matter?" I shouted, as I went through the doorway into the sunshine.

"It's your dog again!" came the gasp of frustration. "He's a total sinner!"

It soon transpired that the young man who had screamed was standing in the middle of the lawn in quite a state of dejection. He had been gently and gratefully unwrapping a sandwich for lunch that had, apparently, been lovingly and caringly put together by his new wife, to sustain him in the heat of the day.

Having examined this token of undying adoration for a little while, he had turned to make some loving comment about the sandwich to one of the others. In doing so, he had lowered his guard and lowered his lunchtime offering to within range of the lolling Labrador licker. Yates had strolled past the dangling morsel, licked it from end to end and walked off a few paces, only to turn, sit, and stare at his prey. The words, "Now what are you going to do?" seemed to hang in the air.

The builder said, "Your dog is plain devious. You know, I've all of a sudden lost my appetite!"

DEVIOUS DEVICES

In order to defeat an enemy, or even a hungry Labrador, it is imperative to understand his *modus operandi*. The defeat of any enemy must, surely, be preceded by an understanding of his tactics. Satan, our great enemy, is the father of lies and a liar from the beginning. His most effective and destructive device is to keep us from seeing the truth about God, about ourselves, and about God's plan of salvation for everyone in the world. Above all, his efforts are intended by him to keep us from seeing the truth about himself and the devastatingly crushing effects of sin.

The subtlety of his approach is to tell us half-truths, so that we might fall into self deception. There is little point in his trying to convince the world that there is no God. Few of us believe that, as creation continuously shouts otherwise. He cannot succeed in convincing many of us that there is no such thing as judgement, because our consciences dictate the opposite. We know that judgement exists —our consciences are God-given, and convict us all the time!

The really cunning approach to sin is to tell people that there is a God and a judgement to come, but then add that there is no hurry. The devil tries to persuade all of us that there is no need to hurry in putting things right with—and turning to—God. The truth is that time is running out fast, and the time to respond to God's calling out to us is always **now**.

The Bible uses three different words to help us gain a clearer understanding of this unpopular subject, and describes its various facets, so that we can hold it up to the light and examine it from different angles.

Firstly, the word 'transgression' means rebellion against

God's laws, making up our own rules and going our own way. Rebellion can be deliberate and wilful or it might be inert and unobtrusive. It could be caused by our saying, 'I am deliberately going to ignore all, or most of, what God says', but, equally, can come about by our saying to ourselves, 'I don't know if God exists anyway, so I simply won't think about these things at all.'

Secondly, the word 'iniquity' is often used of our sinful human nature. It is in our nature to sin. A person is not a liar because he tells lies. He lies because he is a liar. In other words, we are not sinners because we sin, we sin because we are sinners.

The third facet of sin is not so obvious. It is to miss the mark —God's mark, or target. As Paul wrote, 'For all have sinned and fall short of the glory [standard or target] of God' (Romans 3:23). God's target for us is perfection, including completeness, wholeness and maturity. This may seem unfair to the casual observer: God setting a seemingly impossible target, but the standard has not been set by God as something for us to try and attain in our own strength. It is there so that we can be lifted towards it by him, if we are truly open to receiving his healing love. This allows the wonderful possibility of a bottomless well of grace to abound towards us.

Therefore, anything in our lives that falls short of God's standard is also sin. This would include failing to face up to, and resolve, all our hurts from the past; our secret sins, our sins of resentment, pride, anger, bitterness; our failing to resolve our little pockets of immaturity, and so on and so on....

The good news is that we are free to work, with God's help, on overcoming the sins and problems that can so easily engulf us, once the nature of sin and Satan's devices are understood. Without access to the truth about such things as sin and God's redemptive grace, there is no lasting wholeness, little resolution of character issues, and insufficient fellowship with God and other people.

By the way, that sinner Yates won —that time. He ate the sandwich! He had no idea, at that moment, that he was about to be hoisted by his own petard.

With two days to go before the job was done, he was enjoying a final run in the garden before I left for a speaking engagement. There came yet another scream, drifting in through the open back door. Again I rushed out, fearing the worst. Not more sin, surely?

Yates was standing not far away, soaking wet from his nose to the middle of his back, quite miserable and shell-shocked. I put my hand down to comfort him, and found his head to be a sticky, sugary mass of congealing black hair. "What's happened this time?" I enquired of the nearest builder.

"That'll teach him!" he replied. "It's about time he got back some of his own medicine!"

The builders had kept a supply of fizzy lemonade —in the shade of the apple tree and out of reach, on the top of the barbecue. One half finished bottle had been drunk from, and then left on the new patio.

Yates had seen the untidiness, and deftly removed the bottle. That was when it all began to go terribly wrong for him. He walked up to the builder with, "Chase me, chase me!" oozing from every pore. When the only reaction he could elicit from the lemonade owner was a shrug of resignation, Yates shook the bottle vigorously from side to side. As this did not produce the required result of a chasing builder, he shook it again —and again.

Totally frustrated at not being able to provoke a chase, Yates bit deeply into the bottle, releasing the now highly pressurised gas with the noise of a 12-bore shotgun. The lemonade shot everywhere!

"That'll teach you!" I thought, as I took him off to clean him up.

13

Steal Away

..."All men are like grass,
and all their glory is like the flowers of the field;
the grass withers and the flowers fall,
but the word of the Lord stands forever."

And this is the word that was preached to you. Therefore, rid yourselves of all malice and all deceit, hypocrisy, envy, and slander of every kind.

I Peter 1:24–2:1

In other words there is no point in just 'seeming' to be good!

We had a long, hot, car journey one memorable day, to a friend's vicarage in mid-Wales. The weather was boiling! While I sat in the passenger seat with my tongue almost hanging out of the window to keep cool, Yates lay across the whole back seat, oblivious to the heat, the conversation, the fly that came in through the window to join him, and the incessant drone of the engine.

FIND THE WAY!

The temperature that day demanded our stopping for long, refreshing drinks, and those breaks resulted in my arriving at the vicarage in a state of yearning to visit the smallest room in the house!

Our kind host directed me, without delay, to his downstairs facility, which was to the right of a small passage leading away from the far end of the kitchen.

Across the room we marched, Yates and I. We turned left at the end, to go around the large, scrubbed, wooden kitchen table, then past the full length of it, to turn left again towards the passage. Yates marched on without hesitation, apparently only too aware of his master's great need and the urgency of the mission!

The room was too small for both of us —Yates would have to wait for me outside the door.

This was not a problem. Guide dogs are probably the most highly trained dogs at work today and, among a thousand other things, are trained to wait patiently, without moving a muscle, for anything up to ten minutes. This particular feature of the training comes in very handy when a guide dog needs to be found exactly where he was left.

"Wait!" I commanded, and entered the room with reassurance in my heart that he would be there waiting for me, exactly as I had left him. Sure enough, on opening the door, and reaching down with my hand, there was Yates, exactly where I had left him! This dog is so good!

From the other side of the kitchen came a muffled giggle. Did I sense some deception here?

To make my point about little, private deceits I sometimes tell a made-up story about another vicar altogether, who primed up his congregation one Sunday morning, by saying to them, "Next Sunday I want to preach on the subject of lying. As a preparation for the sermon, I should like you all to read the seventeenth chapter of Mark." When the following Sunday arrived, the preacher climbed into the pulpit to begin his sermon, saying, "Now then, would all those who have read the seventeenth chapter of Mark, as I requested, raise your right hand?" Nearly every hand in the congregation went, hesitatingly, up in the air. Then said the preacher, "You are the very sort of people I want to talk to. There is no seventeenth chapter in Mark's Gospel!"

Most of us, with the possible exception of Yates, are not quite so flagrantly deceptive. Personal honesty—being authentic, and not pretending to be something that we are not—is extremely difficult. In fact, if the truth be known, one of the hardest struggles we experience in life is being totally honest with ourselves and about ourselves. This appears to me to be quite ludicrous because if we are not utterly candid with ourselves, there is little hope of our being totally honest with God or with anyone else. The tragedy is that God can only help us to become all that he has planned for us to be, to the extent that we are honest with ourselves and him, facing up to who and what we really are —warts and all. God does his business with the real person, and not with the character we try to be.

"What a wonderful dog you have!" the Vicar chortled. Actually, to be really honest about it, he was splitting his sides at this point.

"What's he been up to now?" I asked.

"He watched you so carefully as you shut the door. He waited to hear the bolt go across, and that was it!"

"That was what?"

"He walked, very sedately, back around the table to

the opposite side of the kitchen, ate the cat's dinner from her bowl on the floor, without so much as a 'by your leave', and then returned, slowly and steadily, back to the lavatory door, taking absolute care to replace himself in exactly the same position, so that you wouldn't notice!"

I knelt down on the floor beside him and put my mouth to his ear. "Yates, my friend, are you being completely truthful with me?"

I was told that he looked at me out of the corner of one eye, but I did not get an answer.

14

Getting a Lift

> *Listen, O heavens, and I will speak;*
> *hear, O earth, the words of my mouth.*
> *Let my teaching fall like rain*
> *and my words descend like dew,*
> *like showers on new grass,*
> *like abundant rain on tender plants.*
>
> Deuteronomy 32:1–2

Perhaps it is quite normal for guide dogs to love swimming in lakes but to hate the rain. Yates will splash for hours in a river, but carefully avoid any puddle on the pavement.

So, going home from work one wet and blustery evening last autumn was a challenge. One of the others from the office had walked out behind me, and laughed at the display of canine reluctance to get going against the horizontal downpour. Taking pity on the dog, he shouted against the wind, "Yates, I'll take you home. My car is at the back of the building. If you stand over there on the corner with your master, I'll be with you in a flash!"

FIND THE WAY!

Obediently and gratefully, Yates and I stood on the corner, with God's abundant rain pouring down our faces and dribbling down our backs.

As soon as the car stopped at the roadside, the dog hurled himself across the gap and stood pointing, with great urgency, at the passenger door handle. Of course, I wrenched the door open and quickly clambered in, splattering my rescuer with water. The soaking dog climbed between my knees and began to saturate my trousers as I pulled the car door shut.

As the car did not hasten onwards at this point, I simply assumed there was traffic crossing in front of us. Turning to my driver, I apologised for the dog drippings that were drenching his carpet, no doubt leaving soggy, doggy patches, awash with wet black hairs.

"Isn't it awful?" I said, over the noise of the thrashing windscreen wipers. "What terrible weather! I'm sorry about the mess on your carpet. I hope I'm not getting the seat too wet."

The driver replied, "Who are you?"

How embarrassing! Wrong car. Right timing—wrong place. To feel completely in the wrong place like that is quite disturbing.

The whole incident lasted no more than a few minutes, but served as a reminder that many have experienced a similar sense of being lost, unwanted, in the wrong place—we might think, for example, of the homeless, or refugees, who are often made to feel rejected and unwanted, in all kinds of ways. The feeling of embarrassment that I experienced, for that brief moment, helped me to imagine the infinitely greater pain of those who are 'displaced', who need, as we all do, a place of acceptance, where they can know that they 'belong'.

GETTING A LIFT

There is a spiritual counterpart to such a sense of 'displacement'. Until we find peace with God and begin to enjoy his loving presence, we cannot truly feel, at the deepest level, that we have found the spiritual home that we need. Jesus wants us to find the one place where we will really belong. Chapter fourteen of St. John's Gospel has much to tell us about this. We can trust Jesus to prepare a place in heaven for us (v.3). He is the ***only*** way for us to come to God the Father (v.6). To know Jesus is to know the Father (v.9). Faith leads us to do the kind of things Jesus did, and more (v.12). Jesus sends the Spirit, to be with the believer for ever (vv.16–17); and we are in Jesus and he is in us (v.20). This assurance is reinforced in verse 23, along with a warning that the cost is obedience: "If anyone loves me, he will obey my teaching. My Father will love him, and we will come to him and make our home with him."

At the very deepest level, we can find our true home only when we come to Jesus in faith. Then we will know where we are, whose we are, and where we are heading.

As we clambered, apologetically, out of the stranger's car, I tried to encourage Yates by telling him that he would have been damp and undesirable company to anyone that night, whether we were in the right car or not, but it did not seem to make any difference. He still looked like a displaced dog —forlorn, bedraggled and miserable in the downpour. He did not look as though he was truly appreciating the abundance of God's grace in delivering all that rain!

15

Adoption

Children's children are a crown to the aged, and parents are the pride of their children.

Proverbs 17:6

There will always be a group of involved parents at a school prize-giving, concert or sports day. If those parents are honest, they would tell us that they have only really come to see one person walk onto the platform to receive a prize, to see one figure sing the song or flash past them on the race-track. They will always, of course, politely applaud the others, but it is only one—their particular one—that they have come to see.

This is wonderfully normal parental behaviour and there is nothing wrong with it. Anything that our own children achieve has many times the thrill for us than something that someone else's child has done.

My children are all grown up and long ago flown the

nest, but I have a much smaller, adopted 'son' now, in the four-legged shape of my guide dog!

Yates took me to the big supermarket in town the other day, to attempt the acquisition of a passport photograph. New and uninteresting bureaucratic regulations were demanding one for a special card that would allow a blind person, or rather someone driving a blind person, to park his car wherever is convenient, often in the special car park slots reserved for disabled people. This necessitated our finding one of those automatic machines that do all the photographic work, in answer to the sensation of receiving money in the slot. The problem was this: how was I to find the photo kiosk? Yates had never been in one before; we have no name for it, and he would not recognise it if he saw it! The command, 'Find the kiosk' would have fallen on puzzled ears. I knew there was one somewhere in the large supermarket foyer, but that was not the same as knowing where to go and asking the dreaded question, 'Is there anyone in here?' I did not want to sit on some dear member of the general public going about their private photographic business!

Yates and I entered the main doors of the shop and stopped by the customer services desk. We negotiated the right amount of small change, but we were back out in the foyer before I realised that I had forgotten to ask where the kiosk was located, or for any help to find it.

"I'm sorry, Yates! How are we going to find this machine now?" At the sound of my voice, he swung suddenly to the right, took four paces forward, and stopped. Tentatively reaching ahead with my right hand, I found, three inches beyond the end of his nose, the empty seat in front of the automatic camera!

ADOPTION

"You wonderful dog!" I rubbed his ears. "What an amazing animal you are! I am thrilled to bits with you!"

God is so often thrilled to bits with his adopted children, too. He is our Father and we are his children, and all the time he looks on and watches what we do. He is not watching in any critical way, ready to shout or condemn. He is watching as any parent watches his child: when the child does something well, it makes the parent glad.

Similarly, God loves each one of us as if there was only one of us to love. Each one of us, therefore, has it in us to bring joy to the heart of God —when we are obedient to him and seek to please him. That is, indeed, something to live for.

> Whom have I in heaven but you?
> And earth has nothing I desire besides you.
> My flesh and my heart may fail,
> but God is the strength of my heart
> and my portion forever.
>
> *Psalm 73:25–26*

Between a guide dog and his owner, one thing above all is noticeable. Once we have got over the, 'Isn't he a beauty!' syndrome, and the, 'Oh, they are such clever dogs!' sensation of wonder, we can begin to see the immense bonding that begins to take place as owner and dog work ever more closely together. The guidance given to me from the GDBA was that it might take a further year after training to achieve the sought-after level of bonding required to enable a full and proper understanding to rise up between the two of us. Well, in Yates' case this has not

FIND THE WAY!

stopped growing. Each week and every month, I become aware of yet tighter feelings, swifter reactions, and extra gentle touching by way of checking up on me —extra dollops of extra care. There are some places, like the office and the garden at home, where I know my way around sufficiently well enough to manage little trips without him. There is hardly anywhere else, however, where I can walk more than a few steps without him, and a greying black nose thrusts itself up into the palm of my hand as if to ask, "Do you know what you're doing, Dad? Do you need any help?"

There are some occasions too, like visiting the theatre, when it is quite safe to leave Yates at home and enjoy an evening on my wife's arm. This sounds fine and is most pleasurable, but returning home needs a preparation and firmness of footing almost beyond human endeavour! Once the key is turned in the back door, eighty pounds of black lightning comes hurtling towards me at something far in excess of any civilised speed limit! The full muscle-and-bone weight of charging dog crashes into the midriff, and only a sturdy, rock-like stance saves me from being tumbled backwards onto the path!

Yates' thrill and excited joy at re-union never fails to bring a little tear to my eyes —it is so intensely sincere. There are no flaws in his adoration. In all his feelings and attentions towards me, Yates is clearly saying, "I am the same through and through." This is a very powerful affirmation. Most of us would have to admit that our sincerity may slip a little at times. Only one person who has lived on this earth was *completely* good and invariably sincere —a person without any flaw, sin or defect at all: his name is Jesus Christ. Those who *receive* him become adopted children of God, born again by the Spirit of God.

> Yet to all who received him, to those who believed in his name, he gave the right to become children of God — children born not of natural descent, nor of human decision or a husband's will, but born of God.
>
> *John 1:12–13*

Then, it is not just that his strength and character are good examples to follow; we are given a new Spirit; we receive the righteousness of Jesus; and the Holy Spirit actually imparts more and more of the character of Jesus, as we go on being filled, and as we learn from the word of God to walk in obedience. God's strength is then sufficient for our needs, and we begin to minister effectively for him, as we start to exercise faith in practical ways. We begin to *behave* as the adopted children we become when we received Jesus.

For a Christian who is walking in obedience to the pure word of God and moving in the flow of the Holy Spirit, though, Jesus Christ is at the heart of life. The believer worships Jesus in his heart, rejoices in, loves and glorifies him ***above all else***. The fellowship, love and approval of Jesus Christ are preferred above all other people, possessions, pleasures, or pursuits. When we receive Jesus, and then walk with him obediently and faithfully, we truly discover for ourselves a joy and peace that nothing and no-one else can give. We truly know that we are adopted children of our loving heavenly Father.

By the same author:

TRUST YATES!
Stories of a Guide Dog with a Dog Collar

Foreword by Adrian Plass

Close your eyes and imagine allowing a dog to guide you safely wherever you go—then you get an idea of the sort of trust that Mike Endicott and many other blind people have to learn.

Yates is a very special guide dog—sensitive, intelligent and greatly loved by people to whom his owner ministers.

In this book, Mike tells of some of the profound truths he has learnt during his time with Yates.

ISBN 1901949087

UK £5.99 $14.95 in Canada

LET HEALING FLOW, LORD

This book tells the amazing story of a vision for Christian healing ministry. Mike Endicott traces the unfolding of that vision—which he describes as being like a 'jigsaw puzzle'. Gradually, the pieces begin to fit together as God's plan unfolds.

The fruit of this has been the founding of the Order of Jacob's Well—an order of Christian healing under the oversight of the Archbishop of Wales, which seeks out, trains and encourages those called to the healing ministry of the Church—and the setting up of 'Wells', centres where healing prayer takes place.

God has touched countless lives through this remarkable ministry and the faithful obedience of Mike Endicott and his team.

ISBN 1901949141

UK £8.99 $22.95 in Canada

HEALING AT THE WELL

Preface by
The Archbishop of Wales

Foreword by
Jennifer Rees Larcombe

The Archbishop of Wales writes:
Mike has emerged as one of the outstanding teachers in the Church here and any reader of this book will at once see why. He is entirely honest about his feelings and struggles; entirely realistic, and often very funny, in his assessment of our dim, human capacities; entirely focused on the goodness of God, so that we are reminded all the time of the dangers of treating God like a heavenly mail-order catalogue, trying to reduce God to our scale of priorities.

What you will read here is both a moving personal story about what disablement can mean for a deeply anointed Christian ministry, and a whole series of profound reflections on the nature of our God and of His healing work.

Everything flows from how we learn the patience to stand under the cross of Jesus, because when we are there we see what he sees, the infinite glory and love of the Father. That is where the healing fountains start.

ISBN 1901949079

UK £7.99 $19.95 in Canada